Scripture quotations are taken from the Holy Bible, New International Version®, NIV®.
Copyright © 1973, 1978, 1984, 2011 by Biblica, Inc.™
Used by permission. All rights reserved worldwide.

ISBNs:
Hardcover: 979-8-9935838-0-8
Paperback (Amazon): 979-8-9935838-1-5
Paperback (Bookstores & Libraries): 979-8-9935838-5-3
E-book: 979-8-9935838-2-2

Cover design: Randy Reynolds
Interior layout: Randy Reynolds

First Edition

Dedicated to those who would rather die poor men and women involved in outreach than rich men and women who declined to reach out. To my Grandmother. For the glory of Jesus Christ.

"Hold High, The Torch!"
Ruth Reynolds (1923 – 2020)

Prologue

Sometimes the toughest realizations come only in the face of the greatest adversity. A few years ago, one of my aunts was diagnosed with breast cancer. A month later my youngest brother noticed blood in his stool. After a colonoscopy procedure, he was informed by his physician that there was a polyp (an early form of cancer) removed. About a month later I, too, found blood in my stool. Due to the recent cancer diagnoses in my family, the fear which immediately nestled upon me was unsettling. I quickly called my physician and made an appointment for a colonoscopy procedure.

My procedure was scheduled roughly forty-five days out. This was the first time I had ever truly looked death square in the face, not knowing if it was coming for me. My soul trembled. I cried. I wept.

All the things that mattered didn't seem to matter as much. All the frivolous things that I had dreamt of experiencing disappeared from thought. All that remained were thoughts of my own ignorance toward God and how, living for myself, I had neglected Him so many times before. This truth hurt deeper than any pain I had ever physically felt.

In my sorrow, God met me with His compassion. He reminded me that before I had ever seen a day on this earth, He had known of and made atonement for my sins through Jesus Christ. The comfort I felt was immense. Because I believed in my heart and confessed with my mouth that Jesus is Lord, He died for me, and God raised Him from the dead, God would treat me as though He is ignorant of my sins.

Ignorant is defined as to lack knowledge (Merriam-Webster's Dictionary). My previous way of living was ignorant of God and His commands. I knew much of what God said in the Bible but often I, like the Apostle Paul, chose to "do what I did not want to do" (Romans 7:15-20). In response, because of Jesus Christ, God's love was ignorant of my sins. It had finally fully registered in my mind that it is as if God never knew I had ever committed a transgression toward Him, even though He knew it all. I came to understand that when God looks at me He does not see me at all. Instead, He sees the pure Holy Spirit that lives in me. He sees His Son. He sees Himself.

With my procedure weeks away and confronted with God's ignorant love, the possibility of death no longer mattered. That is because when it comes to the believer, death does not exist. Death is simply a word that we use to express the absence of life. Since Jesus Christ is "the Way, the Truth, and the Life" (John 14:6) it can be aptly asserted that death is a word we use to describe the absence of Christ.

What is a love so great that the one thing which would cause us to not experience it is the very thing that God would set out to rectify? It is a love that, for those who freely accept it, is completely and intentionally ignorant of the fact that sin even exists.

"In response, because of Jesus Christ,

God's love was ignorant of my sins."

Chapter 1
Ignorant Love

Love is ignorant. This idea of *Ignorant Love* swelled in my heart but I wanted to be sure that it is scripturally based before I shared it with anyone. It is a concept that I was skeptical about at first but after prayer, focus, research, and deep studying I have learned it to be true in every way.

Often, people find themselves falling for or being in relationship with someone whose positive characteristics they accept and whose flaws they merely acknowledge. They eventually home in on the negative things and create a space that degrades some of their closest connections. Ignorant love disagrees with how we go about our handling the everyday happenings within those relationships.

Ignorant love, therefore, means that if you love someone unconditionally, you accept and treat them as though you have no working knowledge of their flaws, faults, and failures. All those things that you do not like about them. I mean, isn't that what Jesus does for all who confess and believe? Christians can live their lives in Christ as though they have never sinned. Jesus forgives and cleanses them from the penalty of sin (1 John 1:7).

Normally, with a title such as Ignorant Love and dealing with how we express love relationally, I would think one would assume to begin from the perspective of self-love. Yes, Love Is Autonomous, and before one can effectively love someone else unconditionally, he must know who he is in Christ. The Bible is clear that he must love himself first (Matthew 22:39), as you cannot love your neighbor as you love yourself unless you love yourself already. This concept will be expanded in the second chapter.

Instead, I open with Ignorant Love because when it comes to love this is where most people find themselves beginning. They try to love others before they learn to love themselves. It is not until the aftermath of failed relationships, broken hearted-ness, and even death that people decide to learn who they are as individuals. It is in the pit of loneliness and despair that many find themselves attempting to accept and love the person they see in the mirror.

It is the year 2025 and commonalities across social media platforms regarding relationships shows just how disconnected we are from one another. There is a plethora of men bashing and women bashing. Women consistently discussing what some regularly call "sassy" men; Men discussing what some have coined 304's. A ton of negativity without a conversational purpose. What is the point of having the conversation if the core of the issue is not being discovered and solutions sought after?

What this says is that people have been attempting to love others but have been hurt. For various reasons, their love

is being returned void. This cripples their desire to love open-
ly and freely, due to their past experiences. They gave their
form of love with reckless abandon and ended up feeling as
though their world came crashing down when they were reck-
lessly abandoned.

The reward of a true and loving relationship is only am-
plified by the amount of risk one is willing to take in order to
see it come to fruition. The greater the risk, the greater the
reward. Maybe that is why God calls for us to take up our
own cross with our very lives (Matthew 16:24, Luke 9:23). The
reward that comes with the risk of vulnerability is a reminder
of the rejoicing that took place in heaven when Jesus made
Himself vulnerable so that you could be with Him. The risk is
set. The penalty of not receiving Christ's gift is immense but
the reward is greater! For that reason, the only choice of sub-
stance that a non-believer can make is the decision to either
live with Christ for eternity or live without Christ for eternity.
Additionally, even as a believer your everyday actions reflect
the choice you made.

Peter's Un-forgiveness

When it comes to people's flaws and faults love shows
itself by treating those people as though they have none. Thus,
true love reveals itself as being as though it is completely un-
aware, or ignorant, of others' flaws. When Peter asked Jesus
how often he should forgive someone (Matthew 18:21-22), I
imagine that he was quite shocked to hear Jesus say that he
should forgive someone as much as they need forgiving.

Jesus did not tell Peter to hold on to a grudge. He encouraged him to acknowledge the fault and forgive. The fact

that He said to forgive "seventy times seven" (meaning, as much as necessary) goes on to express that Peter should not cut others off but continue loving them as much as they need to be loved for the sake of Christ, not for selfish ambition.

Therefore, loving someone has more to do with offering yourself to meet their needs in way that allows them to experience Christ's love through you, instead of you seeking to get what you can out of the relationship. This does not mean that relationships are not mutually beneficial. They are. Allowing ourselves to become vulnerable so that you can meet the needs of others as they meet your needs puts you in a greater position to experience, on an extremely small scale, what God does for you daily as He meets your needs, without a mandate or requirement.

To be clear, this does not mean that Christians should go about sinning and living their life as though they do not have a relationship with God. On the contrary, Christians are set apart. True relationships, especially relationships with God, drive change in the recipient and create a desire to please the other person. Hence, experiencing God's love should, over time, create a greater desire to please Him. In the same way, experiencing the love of someone else should, over time, create a greater desire to please them. As recipients of God's love, you learn to love others as you encounter God daily loving you. He creates the change in you; You choose to replicate it. Your actions are not changed. Your mind and your heart are.

Penalties and Consequences

I am not writing this to say that once you accept Jesus Christ and receive salvation that God no longer cares if you sin or not. God certainly cares about how you live your life. I am saying that, after you accept Christ and receive salvation, there is no eternal separation from God for your sin. Yet, there are consequences for your sin. God loves you, despite you.

The penalty for sin is death (Romans 6:23). In today's language when someone hears the word dead, it is understood to mean that a person is no longer breathing, and blood no longer courses through their veins. A misinterpretation of Romans 6:23 is, your sin will cause you to die. The book of Genesis exposes the truth.

When God first placed Adam in the Garden of Eden, Adam enjoyed a complete and fully connected relationship with God. Adam was warned that he "must not eat from the tree of knowledge of good and evil, for when [he] eats from it [he] will surely die" (Genesis 2:17). To make the long story short, because of Satan's deception when Eve, followed by Adam, ate from the tree of the knowledge of good and evil they did not physically die. Instead, due to their sin they were spiritually separated from God. For the first time, the absence of God in a perfectly connected relationship with Adam was all too real.

Adam and Eve developed a heightened sense of self along with their own shortcomings, as seen in Genesis 3:7 when, "the eyes of both of them were opened, and they realized they were naked." Immediately after their sin, internally the two began to identify themselves with the shame that came from their disobedience. We uncover evidence of this when we read that they sewed fig leaves together to cover their nakedness. The penalty for their transgression was separation from God. The consequence for their sin was shame, guilt, all that God outlined in Genesis 3, and the innate desire to sin

16

being passed on to every person ever born from Adam's seed. But God had a plan.

He Sent His Son

God sent Jesus to restore mankind's relationship with Him. Jesus Christ "bore our sins in His body on the cross" (1 Peter 2:24). "God gave His One and only Son so that whoever believes in Him will not die but have everlasting life (John 3:16)." This does not mean that those who believe will walk the face of the earth for eternity. It does mean that the penalty for your sin, eternal separation from God, was paid for by Jesus Christ on the cross at Calvary. It also means that your previously non-existent relationship with God has been restored. At this point, some of you may ask "if God really loves us, then why is there so much pain in the world?" Well, I'm glad you asked.

Love is ignorant. Love says, "I am aware of your flaws but I look past them because I understand that your flaws do not define you." Who in your life could use a little ignorant love? Whose faults do you choose to see and whose do you choose to look past?

Living a life of love is not easy. It is sometimes stressful and even tiresome. Shucks, sometimes, it's overwhelming in the most draining way. Often, the love one is expected to express is not returned from those it was given to. Regarding this, there are a few important things to note.

First, the Bible never tells us to change anyone. God simply instructs us to plant seeds or water seeds (1 Corinthians 3:6) and to renew our own minds (Romans 12:1-2). God causes the increase, meaning He is the One who changes people. That change doesn't always come in the form of what we expect to see, which is tangible results with the naked eye. Take control of what you have control of.

For instance, when someone accepts Jesus Christ as their Savior, God gives them a new heart. He gives them His heart, spiritually, one that desires to please Him by way of the Holy Spirit. This is done by accepting salvation through faith regarding Jesus' substitutive death and the reception of the Holy Spirit who leads and guides believers toward the likeness of Jesus Christ. But how do you go about loving others when others are so unlovable? Hold on to this question for a minute.

This brings us to the second point: a man cannot adequately say, "I love you" to anyone absent the Holy Spirit through Jesus Christ. Now, before you get all into a tizzy, let me explain.

Merriam-Webster's dictionary defines love as, 1) a feeling of strong or constant affection for a person, 2) attraction that includes sexual desire, 3) the strong affection felt by people who have a romantic relationship. This completely contradicts what God says love is and places love as a feeling of carnal passion that leads to sex. The Bible clearly defines love as this: "God is love" (1 John 4:8). What does this mean in comparison to our modern dictionary's definition?

It means that outside the will of God you cannot express, experience, convey, show, feel, or represent love in any shape, form, or fashion. Your actions must be with godly intent and from the heart in a way that is pleasing, and points, to God. To love someone in the most basic terms possible, is to express God to them. It means to be God's representative to them. It means to convey a godly experience that is going to show Jesus Christ in a positive light and attract others to Him.

This does not mean that you must always be happy-go-lucky with a fake and cheesy smile on your face like some have. You know, or know of, some people like that. The ones that are always so "blessed and highly favored!".

Expressing Jesus to others will mean making tough decisions that will hurt some feelings and sometimes it will mean comforting the person whose feelings you couldn't care less about. If we are honest people, and let's be honest people, you will admit that there are just some people you can't stand. Loving someone doesn't mean liking them. It means showing them Jesus Christ whether you like them or not.

Understanding that your spirituality is that of constant progression is the key to growth in your relationship with Christ. I cannot tell you how many times I have met new believers who have adopted the idea that once you give your life to Jesus you can just take your hands off the wheel (see what I did there?). Jesus is not some control freak that wants to steer the vehicle of your life toward heaven. He's more like a teacher instructing you how to drive the vehicle of your life as His Holy Spirit guides you to the places and people God has set for you. He understands that this a journey, a faith journey, through life full of hazards, obstacles, roadblocks, failures, successes, joys, fast tracks, and legacy. But in our twenty-first century society there is this unsaid underlying idea that, "I am an adult, and my life is already busy enough. What I need for my spirituality needs to be delivered on Sunday morning and Wednesday night."

You cannot become the servant of tomorrow feeding those which God has placed under your responsibility without first drinking spiritual milk today (1 Corinthians 3:2). Just as every newborn baby develops at different rates and speeds, so every Christian develops at various rates and speeds. Similarly, as babies are needy for breastmilk as the basis for their survival so are Christians needy for spiritual milk as the basis for their survival. The only difference between those babies and Christians is this: Babies actively seek out the things that will help them live while Christians often actively walk away from the things that will help them live. The basis for all Christians, the crux of our entire faith, is Jesus Christ and our need for Him.

"In response, because of Jesus Christ,
God's love was ignorant of my sins."

Chapter 2
Love Is Autonomous

Imagine you are a five-year-old child. Like most children that age you are steadily venturing through your surroundings trying to figure out how things work, what you are capable of, and how best to interact with things and people around you. Some things work well while others do not. Sometimes you push the boundaries with the limits that have been set by parents and sometimes you do not. With the extent to which you are not corrected you continually press forward pushing boundaries learning that you are your own boss. By experience, you learn that you are autonomous in the sense that you learn how best to be based on your own experiences, your own personality, and your own skills. Over time you need less and less help with things because you can "do it on your own." Not only do you feel you do not need the help, but you also do not want it.

At around that age, something else begins to form quietly in the heart of a child: a belief system about strength and weakness. When a five-year-old says, "I can do it myself," what they are really saying is, "I want to feel strong. I want to feel capable. I want to feel like I matter." That phrase, innocent as it sounds, is often the earliest expression of a craving for identity.

The child does not yet know that certain tasks are too heavy or too dangerous. They simply know that, so far, no one has stopped them from trying. If they reach for the hot stove and no hand gently pulls them back, they learn a dangerous lesson: "If nobody corrects me, it must be okay." If they run wild without boundaries and no one redirects them, another lesson begins to write itself on their heart: "I set my own limits. I answer to me."

So, by pure experience, they conclude that independence equals safety and needing help equals weakness. They learn that to be praised is to perform well and to be scolded is to be "bad." This is how, unintentionally, experience starts shaping identity long before truth has the chance to.

Now, imagine that same pattern carried into adulthood. Imagine learning about life, love, and identity the same way you learned about walking and talking: mainly through trial and error, trial and pain, trial and confusion. You continue to push relational and moral "stoves" without ever truly asking if they are burning you. You continue to run through life without boundaries because no one ever taught you what a godly boundary looks like. You continue to believe, "If no one stops me, this must be fine," and "If I survived it, it must have been good for me.

The problem is not the desire to grow. The problem is that autonomy without guidance always leads to distortion. A five-year-old can learn to pour a cup of juice eventually, but you would never hand them the keys to a car. Yet spiritually and emotionally, many of us grabbed the keys to our lives long before we learned how to drive them.

That childhood illusion of "I've got this" quietly grew up with you. It just changed languages. It turned into phrases like, "I don't need anyone," "I can heal myself," "I know what's best for me," and "I'll figure it out on my own." What began as a developmental phase became a spiritual posture: a posture that pushes God's hand away in the very areas where we need His touch the most.

Sadly, we treat God and love for self the same way. We treat ourselves as though we are the best teachers at learning how to love ourselves. We venture out into our surroundings trying to figure out things like, "How do I fit in? What am I capable of? How do I best interact with things and people in order to receive the most enjoyment and fulfillment?" Now, I know most of you are not walking around literally asking these things. But by your actions, each of you have inadvertently figured, or tried to figure, these things out for yourself. The proof is in how you see yourself. Just think about it.

Time and again you have gotten into relationship after relationship attempting to decipher the best ways not to get hurt. You search for ways to please your potential mate at the sacrifice of your own feelings and emotions. In the event of a breakup you are left wondering, "What did I do wrong? I did everything for them. What's wrong with me?" These self-reflection questions and statements are just a small fraction of the things that people ask themselves after a terrible breakup. Yet, the point remains the same.

If you were to slow those relationships down like a movie in slow motion, you would see the same scenes playing out over and over again with different faces and different names.

At the beginning, there is excitement. Someone finally notices you, chooses you, and gives you attention. The feeling is electric. You feel seen, wanted, and maybe even special.

Then, little by little, you begin to reshape yourself to keep that feeling. You laugh at things that aren't funny just to keep the mood light. You swallow your discomfort when something bothers you because you don't want to seem "needy." You overextend yourself to prove you're worth keeping. You ignore red flags because you're afraid of being alone again. This is not weakness. It is searching. Searching for a sense of worth that you cannot provide yourself.

When the relationship falls apart, the pain is about more than losing that person. It feels like you lost your reflection. "If they left," you think, "does that mean I'm not lovable? Not beautiful? Not enough?" And because they held the mirror, you assume the problem is the person in the reflection, not the mirror itself.

So, you adjust. You tell yourself, "Next time, I'll be more patient. Next time, I'll be less demanding. Next time, I'll be more understanding. Next time, I'll give even more of myself." You try to "upgrade" yourself not according to God's standard, but according to what the last person did or did not like about you.

This is how an entire identity can quietly be constructed out of rejection and disappointment. You build your sense of self around avoiding pain instead of around God's truth. You become an expert at preventing abandonment but a stranger in authentic love.

And here is the painful reality: Even if someone stayed, as long as your worth is tied to their presence, you would never feel secure. The slightest change in tone, the slightest delay in text messages, the smallest disagreement would shake the foundation of who you think you are. Because people, even well-meaning people, were never meant to be your foundation.

Your heart has been using relationships like a mirror, but the mirror is cracked. And a cracked mirror can never give you a clear reflection.

Too often people take a negative view of self, based on how others have treated or better yet, mistreated them. The more negative experiences you have with others, the more likely you are to develop a distorted view of self because it seems that the only constant in each relationship is the person you see in the mirror. So how do you eliminate the negative views that permeate your head? The answer can be found in Colossians 3.

From the Apostle Paul's letter, the people of Colossi are taught that there are practical things they can do to overcome their distorted thoughts and view of self. "If then you were raised with Christ, seek those things which are above, where Christ is, sitting at the right hand of God. Set your mind on things above, not on things on the Earth. For you died, and your life is hidden with Christ in God" (Colossians 3:1-3).

First, Paul reminds you that you have the authority to seek the eternal realities of Heaven (v1). Second, he gives direction on how to do so when he wrote, "Set your mind on things above, not on things on the Earth" (v2). He rounded this out with why you should do so with, "For you died, and your life is hidden with Christ in God" (v3). What is there to learn from this?

When Paul tells you to "seek those things which are above" and to "set your mind on things above," he is not asking you to ignore your pain, your bills, your family drama, your past, or your present struggles. He is not saying, "Pretend it doesn't exist." Instead, he is teaching you where to anchor your identity in the middle of it.

Think of your mind like the lens on a camera. Whatever you focus the lens on becomes the clearest part of the picture. Everything else blurs into the background. When your lens is set on earthly things—people's opinions, personal failures, past mistakes, cultural standards—those things become the sharpest part of how you see yourself. God's truth becomes blurry in the background.

Paul is saying to change what's in focus. "Set your mind" is a deliberate act. It means to fix, anchor, and stabilize your thoughts in one direction. It is the intentional choice to make God's view of you the clearest, sharpest, most dominant reality in your mind, even when everything in your life is screaming something different.

That's why he reminds you, "For you died, and your life is hidden with Christ in God." Your "old you," the one shaped purely by experience, trauma, and opinion, died with Christ. The version of you that constantly questions your worth, that fears rejection, that clings to people for validation...that identity is not the one God is looking at.

The real you is "hidden with Christ in God." That means that the true version of you is wrapped up in who Jesus is. Your identity is inseparable from Him. Your value is secure because it is stored in Him, not in human approval. Your destiny is protected because it is anchored in His purpose, not your performance.

So when you begin the process of comparing your thoughts to God's Word, you are not adding something foreign. You are uncovering what is already hidden in Christ. You are not trying to become someone else; you are learning to live like who you already are in Him.

You take the thoughts which you have, then you compare them with what God says in the Bible and God's character. If your thoughts do not line up with God's word and His character, then you have a choice to make. Either continue to accept and behave the same ways that you have and disregard what God says. Or, you can put down the thoughts, views, and behaviors that you created and accepted about yourself and adopt the thoughts and views that God gave you and behave accordingly. Let's take a look at how that reveals itself in our everyday life. Let's make it personal because it is a bad thing for a Christian to look in the mirror and see anything less than what God sees. The following is a practical exercise that you can do, and share with others, to help this hit home.

Make It Tangible

Take a sheet of paper. On the front of that sheet of paper, list the following categories down the side of the paper: Emotionally, Mentally, Physically, Spiritually. Now, using a number scale of 1 through 10, with 10 being the best, rate yourself in each category on how well you see yourself. If you are like me then each individual number is less than ten. On average, my score was six.

What this says about you is, "I am not where I am supposed to be or where I could be." Hold that thought. Now, turn your paper over to the reverse side.

On the reverse side of your paper, list those same categories down the side of the page (Emotionally, Mentally, Physically, Spiritually). Next, I want you to rate Jesus in each one of these categories ranging on a scale of 1 through 10. If you are like me then each number is ten. If it is not ten, then I am sure that the numbers you gave for Jesus are higher than yours. That is the important thing. But there is a major issue with what results this exercise presents. The results of this exercise reveals that, as a Christian who has been saved through Jesus' sacrifice, you still identify with who you used to be more than you identify with Jesus, even after receiving the gift of salvation.

You look in the mirror at yourself and you still see the three. You still see the six. You still see whatever number you gave yourself and you identify with it. You identify with it to the point where you cannot fathom how God could look at you and see anything more than the mess of your sins. How could this great, perfect, omnipotent God see you and think to Himself, "I am pleased."?

In contrast, you marked Jesus at higher rates than yourself because you know of, or understand, His perfection. For, "He committed no sin, and no deceit was found in His mouth" (1 Peter 2:22). You understand that but you do not, or have not fully accepted, the truth that when God looks at you, He no longer sees that three. He no longer sees that six.

Instead, He sees the perfection of Christ that lives in you! He sees the ten! So, why do you continue to look at yourself and see anything less than what He sees? If God looks at you and identifies you with Himself, why do you look at yourself and not identify with Christ who lives in You through the Holy Spirit? The autonomy of love is that in order to love yourself freely, without outside influence, you must first admit that you do not know how. God's love must be the anchor through which your perception is grounded.

Every Christian should return to the mirror exercise often—not to measure their sin, but to confront the places where their identity is still shaped by something other than Christ. When you compare the numbers you give yourself with the numbers you give Jesus, the gap is not an indictment. It is a diagnosis. It exposes the places where you're still clinging to an old version of yourself, the places where wounds have become labels, the places where shame still whispers in the background, and the places where childhood conditioning still shapes your sense of worth.

But here is the truth: You cannot embrace the mind of Christ while still holding onto the mirror of your past.

This exercise isn't about calling you unworthy. It is about showing you where you've accepted a lie. A lie, believed long enough, becomes a personal truth, even when it contradicts God's truth. Many Christians don't struggle because they lack faith; they struggle because their reflection is still tied to who they used to be. They can believe Jesus is perfect, but they can't fully imagine God seeing them through that same perfection.

So instead of seeing this exercise as a comparison, see it as clarity. The numbers don't expose how far you fall short. They expose where God wants to lift you up. They reveal where your identity still needs healing. They pinpoint the parts of you that still operate from insecurity instead of inheritance. And once you see the gap, you can partner with God to close it—not through striving, but through surrender.

Because growth doesn't happen when you try harder; it happens when you agree with what God has already said about you. And once you begin to agree with God about who you are, the mirror changes. Slowly, the reflection shifts. Slowly, the old self loses its grip. Slowly, the identity of Christ becomes the identity you recognize.

This is the beginning of spiritual transformation: not performing for God, but finally seeing yourself the way God already sees you.

Do you remember when I said that it is a bad thing for a Christian to look in the mirror and see something less than what God sees? Learning who you are through life experience alone is a hindrance in connecting with the identity God has set for you.

Life will try to teach you who you are before God ever gets the chance to speak. The world does not wait for you to grow. It begins shaping you the moment you are born. You learn to protect yourself long before you learn to trust God. You learn to survive before you learn to surrender. You learn to perform before you learn to rest. The patterns you absorb from experience become the patterns you believe are normal, even when they were never meant to be your identity. When you look back at the years that formed you, you begin to realize that the loudest voices were not always the most truthful ones. Some voices taught you fear. Some taught you insecurity. Some taught you shame. Yet God always intended for His voice to be the one that shaped you. When life becomes the teacher instead of the classroom, you end up mistaking survival skills for identity. God never asked you to become who your experiences demanded. He asked you to become who He designed. Then to use your experiences to help people get from where you were, to where He is.

Society reinforces the older identity long after God has begun working on the new one. Culture teaches you to prove yourself, to earn worth, to gather affirmation as if approval were a currency. You become conditioned to measure yourself by productivity, performance, appearance, and reputation. You learn to adapt rather than transform. You learn to hide rather than heal. Society invites you to wear masks tailored for acceptance and then praises the mask while ignoring the soul behind it. Over time, these layers become heavy. You start believing you must maintain every version of yourself you ever created just to be understood. Yet none of these versions reflect who God is calling you to be. The pressure to meet expectations becomes the source of confusion. You cannot find your true self while trying to satisfy a world that never knew who you were in the first place.

Generational patterns add another layer to the struggle. You inherit tendencies that were never addressed. You absorb pain that was never healed. You repeat behaviors that were never questioned. Families hand down both blessings and burdens, and many burdens go unspoken for so long that they begin to feel like destiny. You watch your parents navigate life and you learn silently. You watch how they handle stress, conflict, love, and anger, and you carry their habits without even noticing. These patterns shape the rhythm of your reactions. They tell you how to think, how to respond, how to interpret love, and how to guard your heart. But generational patterns are not divine instructions. They are simply echoes of human experience. When you begin to walk with God, He confronts the patterns that have guided you and replaces them with truth. What you inherited does not have to become what you pass down.

This is the heart of breaking every chain. A chain is anything that ties you to a version of life God never endorsed. Chains hold tight because they are familiar. They wrap themselves around your emotions, your memories, and your sense of normal. Sometimes chains feel more comfortable than freedom because freedom requires transformation. Breaking a chain means confronting the part of you that would rather stay the same. It requires honesty about who you are becoming instead of who you have been. God does not break chains to shame you. He breaks them to show you what was possible all along. Each breakthrough is an invitation to step into a life that reflects His love rather than your fears. The moment the chain snaps, you learn that the prison was never as strong as the hope God planted inside you.

Going M.A.D. which is living with the intention to Make A Difference is not about striving. It is about alignment. You impact the world most when you live from the identity God restored rather than the identity life created. You are not called to impress people. You are called to carry light. Influence is the natural result of obedience. When your heart shifts from survival to surrender, your presence becomes a ministry. The way you forgive becomes a testimony. The way you love becomes a message. The way you walk through pain becomes a blueprint for someone else's healing. Making a difference does not happen because you try harder. It happens because you become who you were always meant to be.

This leads into the purpose God placed within every person. Purpose is not an assignment you must complete. It is the expression of the identity God formed inside you. When you understand who you are in Him, your life becomes a reflection of His intention. Purpose flows from identity, not pressure. You were created to carry God's image into the world through your character, your compassion, your creativity, and your convictions. Purpose shows up in the way you treat people, the way you speak, the way you give, the way you endure, and the way you trust. It is woven into the small moments as much as the major ones. When you walk in purpose, you no longer chase validation. You walk with clarity because you know your life is part of something eternal.

This is the truth of it all. Everything God has spoken over you has been consistent from the beginning. You were never meant to live confused. You were never meant to be defined by wounds. You were never meant to carry the weight of past mistakes as if they were permanent labels. God has been calling you back to your real identity since the first moment you strayed from it. The truth is simple. You are loved more deeply than you understand. You are held by a grace that does not weaken. You are guided by a God who has never lost sight of who you are, even when you did. The truth frees you because it restores you. When you embrace God's truth, your entire life begins to align with the hope that has been waiting for you.

Be reminded daily that the journey of becoming is not a path you walk alone. God is patient with your process. He is faithful through your struggle. He is unwavering in His love. Every day you move closer to the version of yourself that reflects His heart. Hold on to that hope. Let it steady your steps. Let it strengthen your choices. Let it comfort you when old patterns call your name again. You are becoming who God always knew you were. You are stepping into a life shaped by truth rather than fear. You are growing into the identity He secured through Christ. Press forward with confidence. Lift your head with expectation. Hold high the torch of faith and let its light guide you home.

Don't be like Adam just after his eyes were opened. You received salvation and still identify with who you used to be instead of who Christ is in you. The reason that is the case is because you have yet to learn who Jesus is as a person, instead of simply your Savior. Knowing Jesus as Savior is wonderful.

It is the first step in living out this life in His image but what next?

The term Christian simply means, "Like Christ". If you are a Christian then you cannot be like most and act as though you have been accepted into some exclusive frat only made available to the blessed and highly favored. At the point of salvation, you must begin to learn who Jesus Christ, the God-man, is. You must learn about how He lived and why. You must learn specifics and principals about how to handle situations that arise and the meaning behind it all… love. In doing so, you will learn to identify less with how you see yourself and more with how you see Him and who He is.

Societal Conditioning

Men are not used to receiving the type of affection that comes with unconditional love. This is a good reason a lot of them cannot give affection or have committed relationships. They do not know how. When they are shown how, they feel uncomfortable as though it is not right. There is nothing wrong with receiving love like this at all. It is the affection every mother and father would give their son or daughter and should be the example we learn to express and expect to receive. You must love your kids at home so they will not search for it in the wrong places after they leave.

There may be more truth to this than we are willing to personally acknowledge. The way a child is raised (qualities, characteristics, morals, acceptable social interactions) is too often decided by how that child perceives what he sees. There is not enough intentional shaping, molding… I mean, discipling (see what I did there?) and children end up becoming a reflection of the world around them. A flawed perception of what they could be. You, as well as myself, have been allowed to fall into this pit of lies that has been accepted as the truth about ourselves.

The primary concern is not what you see when you look at yourself. The most important thing is why you see yourself the way you do because this allows you to attack the root. Your actions are simply an outpouring of the truths you have accepted about yourself. Understanding why you believe something allows you the opportunity to relay, or alter, what you believe. Think about it.

One major complaint that women have about men when in relationships is that men do not know how to express their emotions. Men regularly have issues finding common ground with women in the area of feelings. If this is a major issue, to change it you need to know why it happens in the first place. There is a major clue contributing to understanding in the second commandment that God gave:

> *"You shall not make for yourself an image in the form of anything in heaven above or on the earth beneath or in the waters below. You shall not bow down to them or worship them; for I, the Lord your God, am a jealous God, punishing the children for the sin of the parents to the third and fourth generation of those who hate me, but showing love to a thousand generations of those who love me and keep my commandments" (Exodus 20:4-6).*

This scripture is vitally important to the success or failure of relationships, and growth in relationship with God. Simply put, humans idolize each other. We place each other on pedestals and vainly call each other things like, "King,

Queen, or Princess". I do not believe that people do so maliciously, but I do recognize that these types of happenings contribute to our unwillingness, or inability, to see ourselves the way that God sees us and what God called us to be. We are His servants. "Let a man so consider us, as servants of Christ and stewards of the mysteries of God" (1 Corinthians 4:1).

Yet, odds are that if someone called any of us, "servant", there would likely be an uproar. We are not taught to serve one another, and we are not taught how to be in service to one another. Instead, we are taught to be served and to be serviced. Our language toward each other supports this notion... King... Queen... Princess. Principally, it is the answer to the question "Why are men so out of touch with women when it comes to feelings and emotions." We have made ourselves the idol which God told us not to make. Let's break it down.

The Israelites were warned about what would happen if they allowed some teaching that opposes God's will to hold their attention. If they created and worshipped anything other than God then they would be cursed to the third and the fourth generation. Now, granted, God does not deal with us the same way He did with the Israelites of the Old Testament (Thank God!) but, principally, we still experience the curses spoken of in this chapter. Here is one example of what that looks like:

It is common for a young boy today to be taught at an early age that boys do not cry. His parents and guardians tell him things like, "Stop crying, stop being a punk. Crying is for girls." But when it comes to anger and frustration little boys are allowed to fully explore and express a wide array of intensity. On the other hand, those emotions that are considered soft like sadness, fear, joy, etc. are frowned upon. Young boys are raised to be "strong" and "tough" through hard emotions at the expense of soft ones, as opposed to being taught how to handle all of their emotions without compartmentalizing ones over others. To what extent does this reach into their lives and ability to communicate with others, especially women?

Fast forward twenty years. That little boy from before is nearing his thirties but he cannot keep a steady relationship because he is so out of touch with the women he dates. They are too emotional for him and, from their perspective, he is not emotional enough. The child who was never taught how to healthily express and understand the vast array of emotions God gave him eventually becomes a man who does the same and raises his own children in his likeness. Thus, progressing this curse to the third and fourth generation because his children will be boys who are out of touch with their emotions who grow up to be men without learning how to properly work through problems or communicate with others, especially women.

You cannot raise a boy to be out of touch with his emotions and then expect him to grow up to be a man that is aware of how they affect him and his personal relationships. Little boys must be raised to learn the qualities and characteristics you desire to see them express as men. Not doing so sets boys, especially young black boys, up for failure in many areas and relationships. It is much of what separates man from woman and is often the thing that separates a father from his children. He must learn how to handle the full gamut of his emotions so that he is not overtaken or consumed by them. He cannot conquer an enemy he does not recognize. Discovering early in life how to positively process and express himself will place him in key positions to subdue the overpowering nature of emotions. He can suppress them when necessary to tackle immediate situations but he will not be controlled by them.

In contrast, a little girl with coarse and curly hair who never hears, "Your hair is beautiful. You have good hair." but hears those things being spoken to girls with straight or wavy hair instead is likely to develop the understanding that she does not have good hair. In fact, she is much more versatile and beautiful than she knows. But she has learned, by no fault of her own, that these parts of her are ugly, or not appealing to others.

Children do not inherently see themselves as ugly. They learn what is beautiful, and what is not, by how people treat them in reference to how they interpret the ways others are treated in comparison. Because they are not generally taught an accurate view of self from God's perspective, the only thing left to do is to create their own image or take on the one their parents give them. The sad part is, they do not recognize it.

Understanding what you believe about yourself is the first step. Next is learning why you believe those things. You have been conditioned by how you were raised, experiences in relationships, and experiences you have had by a society that has chosen to worship itself instead of the God that created all things in His image. The God who says, "Do not call anything impure that God has made clean" (Acts 10:15). The identity you resonate most with is the one you have a greater experience with. Knowing that, how can you use this information to increase your identifying with what, who, and whose God says you are? I will give you a hint: Time and energy.

The more time you spend with God, in His word, and building relationship with Him, the more you will identify with Him. Putting off the old you and putting on Christlikeness is a process, one that will take a lifetime of pursuit. It is not easy because it is not familiar. Just remember, this is as much a practical walk as it is a faith walk. Prayerfully, you are receiving the tools in this book as ones for your own kit for daily use as well as clarity to pass it along. You've got this because God's got you! It doesn't matter how slow you go, just don't stop moving forward.

Break Every Chain

There's a beautiful song that was performed by singer Tasha Cobbs titled Break Every Chain. If you have not heard it, I suggest you take the opportunity to give it a listen because it will likely move you as it did me. The lyrics speak of the power that rests in Jesus to break any and every chain that binds us. All those things we get ourselves into that we know we have no business being involved in.

For the non-believer, they are still bound by the chains of sin. For the Christian, one who has received the free gift of salvation, Jesus has already broken every chain. He did that two thousand plus years ago. When referencing self, for one who has accepted salvation, asking Jesus to break every one of your chains is to effectively say, "What He did two thousand years ago was not enough." The important thing to request from God is to help you walk in the freedom from bondage that He's already given you. You cannot be bound by that which you have been freed from! For, Jesus clearly stated to the Pharisees:

"The works I do in my Father's name testify about Me, but you do not believe because you are not My sheep. My sheep listen to My voice; I know them and they fol-low Me. I give them eternal life, and they shall never

perish; no one will snatch them out of My hand. My Father, who has given them to Me, is greater than all; no one can snatch them out of My Father's hand. I and the Father are one" (John 10:25-30).

I believe many people catch the ever-popular verse, "I give them eternal life, and they shall never perish; no one will snatch them out of My hand", and they miss two very important things that were mentioned just before. First, Jesus states, "My sheep listen to My voice".

This basically says that Christians have a relationship with Jesus to the point where they can understand His voice, the Holy Spirit, when He speaks. Second, He says, "[My sheep] follow Me." This means that Christians, true Christians, learn who Jesus is and model their lives after Him. Why is this vital? Well, I am glad you asked.

In order to experience the freedom of autonomous love you must first acknowledge that your view is distorted. You then must base your view of yourself in a constant, an absolute. God, in His omniscience, is the only one whose mind is absolute so you must base your view of yourself through the eyes of the omniscient Father.

Since the Holy Spirit is God's messenger, you must learn how to obey the voice of God by developing a knowledge and understanding of God's Word as well as clarity in hearing God's voice. In doing so, you will learn that God has already broken every chain, that you can walk free of bondage and choose to live a life that is not grounded in the person you used to be, the person you rated less than 10.

True freedom is being able to choose to obey God without penalty of death, death being eternal separation from

God. You recognize that you still have the urges of Satan's lies being whispered in your ear. Yet, despite the desires of your flesh, you choose what aligns with God's character and word. This is an example of free-will. This is a life free of bondage, free of chains, and it is contingent on God sacrificing His only begotten Son, Jesus, on Calvary's hill.

Go M.A.D.

Everyone wants to make a difference in the world somehow. Whether it is being able to help others out, impact the masses, or experience success all major accomplishments involve two things: help from others and personal growth.

It is okay to struggle with seeking outside help and assistance. After all, we are creatures of conditioning. When you have been hurt and let down time after time it becomes much harder to lean on others for the help you very well need in order to grow and/or succeed. So, what if your desire is to impact the world, to make a difference, to "Go M.A.D."?

You spend countless hours becoming a better you by increasing your knowledge, learning new skills, and preparing for feats you have yet to accomplish. No doubt, this is great and should be done. Learn your craft. Become the best you can be at it. But also understand that you must work with others to reach your goal, whatever that goal may be.

You cannot make a difference without an audience. Regardless of the talent, invention, skill, knowledge, or wisdom you obtain through your life's endeavors, if there is no recipient then you may as well have never developed those skills or refined those talents in the first place.

Also, there are many other outside influences, mentors, and examples that you glean from to reach your own goals. Making a difference in the world or in a life, even your family's lives, involves first becoming a better you. There is no better you to model yourself after than Jesus! The more like Christ you become, the more you develop your skills, knowledge, and talents, the better prepared you are to give to others and serve as Jesus served.

Sadly, in our society, we do not place a high value on spiritual development. The major priorities in our lives have become centered around the tangible, material, and things of possession or experience. Even learning how to express emotions in healthy ways has become secondary to what someone owns, has access to, or accomplished. One truth I have learned throughout my life is that true riches come in the form of things you cannot see. A man that can teach someone how to honestly live in a way that can change lives and move hearts is a much richer man than one that has earned millions of dollars. Yes, money speaks, but it only speaks for a time, and sometimes just for a season. It is here today and gone tomorrow.

But what never loses value is the impact you can make in someone by seeing them as someone worth pouring into. To be able to do that, it is critically important that you see yourself as someone worth developing, worth preparing for the opportunity to positively influence someone else. No more looking in the mirror and seeing the person you used to be. It is time to start looking at the perfection that God put inside of you, Jesus Christ.

God's Intended Purpose for Mankind

Ask nearly any Christian what man's "role" is and they will likely tell you one of a few things: 1) Man is the head (leader) of the family and 2) man is supposed to provide. They will use various scriptures to support their stance on the matter. People have accepted this view for themselves without doing their just research on the topic.

What did God say to man when He created him? For what purpose did God create man? Grab your Bible and turn to Genesis 2:15. And it reads, "The Lord God took the man and put him in the Garden of Eden to work it and take care of it."

Now, trust me, I get it. I could see how someone could look at this and say to themselves, "God gave Adam work. See, Adam is a provider." That, contextually, is just not true. If Adam was created to be the provider, then what was Adam in Genesis 2:15 providing for? Eve had not been created at that moment. There was no sin in the world, so Adam enjoyed a perfect relationship with the Father. What need did Adam have to provide?

He did not have a need to provide because he was not created to provide. God is the Provider. God provided everything that Adam would ever need. God also did not give Adam "work". He made Adam steward over all that He provided. God, in all of His goodness, then told Adam how to steward over everything when He said, "Take care of it." Essentially, what God gave Adam was responsibility. But for this to be true here, it must also be true in other parts of scripture, as God's Word rings true while staying consistent.

What are men "except servants, through whom [others

come] to believe—as the Lord has assigned each his task" (1 Corinthians 3:5)? Adam enjoyed complete and perfect union with God. Post sin, God's plan was to reconnect man with Himself. In this process, man's role remains the same: Be a good steward of what God provides. A good modern-day explanation of Adam is as follows.

Essentially, Adam was a farmer who, after sin, lived in a dying world. If you know anything about farming, you understand that it takes meticulous preparation, back-breaking long hours of hard work, and patience in order to receive even the smallest crop. Adam still had the direction from God to "take care of the land" but now it was going to be an intensive process.

When Adam sinned, he did not just lose his connection with God. He also lost his sense of purpose and the role God had for him. He had to find his own way, experientially, and this sinful creation eventually came up with his own view of who he should be and what role he plays. Through the years he even developed a god-like attitude about himself. We see this truth played out in today's society more-so than ever. Remember, we see man's role as one of few things: 1) leader and 2) provider. We see man the way we should see our Father in heaven. It is just as the serpent said to Eve, "...you will be like God..." (Genesis 3:6).

Jesus Christ never told man to lead anything. Instead, He says, "follow Me" (Matthew 10:38). Therefore, He is the leader. Jesus Christ never told man to provide anything. Instead, he says, "If [abundantly] is how God clothes the grass of the field, which is here today and tomorrow is thrown into the fire, will He not much more clothe you, O you of little faith?" (Matthew 6:28). Therefore, God is the Provider. God and Jesus are one. Therefore, God is both leading us to Himself whilst

47

providing for us. Still, Jesus gives us directions. "Therefore, go and make disciples of all nations, baptizing them in the name of the Father and of the Son and of the Holy Spirit, and teaching them to obey everything I have commanded you" (Matthew 28:19). As God did for Adam, so Jesus does for all those who believe. He gives responsibility.

To top it all off, the Apostle Paul reminds us that we are nothing but servants who plant seeds or water seeds (1 Corinthians 3:5) and that God provides the increase. God, the Father, has provided you with any number gifts that are to be used to advance His kingdom and reconnect others to Himself, as He did with you. This comes through various forms and opportunities.

God knows you need money, so He provides you with a job or career. God knows all you need and provides either the occasion or the opportunity for you to grab hold of it. Just as He sent Adam out to take care of all that He provided, He sends you out in similar fashion. It takes hard work. It takes much effort. But being a good steward has its benefit and its reward, some earthly; some heavenly.

You are not the leader! The Holy Spirit is the leader who is guiding us to Christlikeness as Jesus leads us to God. You are Christ's follower as He leads you (John 14:6). All Christians are Christ's followers. Let us move away from this distorted view that our experiences have taught us we are as men and let us return to the purpose and intent God gave to us. In doing so, we will ever-more strongly walk in His power, the power He has given us, to take care of all that He provides.

The Truth of It All

Jesus never said to change the world. Making a difference is all that He ever asked you to do. He said it when He stated, "Therefore go and make disciples of all nations, baptizing them in the name of the Father and of the Son and of the Holy Spirit, and teaching them to obey everything I have commanded you. And surely, I am with you always, to the very end of the age" (Matthew 28:19-20).

Making a difference does not mean that you need to have a large pot of money. The disciples surely did not have an extreme amount of funds supporting them. It means sharing the only thing that has eternal value to all people. The disciples took the necessary time to develop and prepare for the tasks ahead of them and though they are dead, their words still live.

All other kings, emperors, and rulers of that time no longer have the riches of, or the power in, their family bloodline that they amassed during their lifetime. To compare, the richness of a relationship with God and the power offered to those who choose to become a part of Jesus' family are still being passed on to this very day. Now that you have received these riches and power, what are you doing, or going to do, with it in order to ensure that it does not die with you? Do not be like the kings and emperors of old. Be like the disciples and intentionally seek development and growth spiritually, physically, mentally, and emotionally. Let your words and your actions be words that go beyond your lifespan by drawing nearer to and learning more about the person of Jesus Christ. Follow Him.

If you are made in His image then your perspective cannot be, "What can I do for God?". Instead, it needs to be, "What can God do through me?". Jesus is your anchor, and He must be the center-focus, and lens, through which you see yourself and the world. You are made in His image. You are one with the Father and the Son and the freedom to love self, the Autonomy of Love, is grounded in the love of God, Jesus Christ. This truth stands to extend through eternity and so can you.

"You see, at just the right time, when we were still powerless, Christ died for the ungodly. Very rarely will anyone die for a righteous person, though for a good person someone might possibly dare to die. But God demonstrates His own love for us in that: While we were still sinners, Christ died for us" (Romans 5:6-8).

There is no greater reason to better yourself, no greater reason to share with someone else, no greater reason to love and adore God and desire to please Him! Be reminded daily and press on toward that Hope that awaits you. Be encouraged and "Hold High, The Torch" (Ruth Reynolds, 2020)!

"*The autonomy of love is that in order to love yourself freely, without outside influence, you must first admit that you do not know how. God's love must be the anchor through which your perception is grounded.*

Chapter 3
Love Is Intentional

Have you ever ran into someone after an extended period of time of not seeing them and they are just a small portion of who they used to be? What was it that caused them to change from who you remember them being to who they were at that new moment? Think back to the first chapter where it was said, "It is not until the aftermath of failed relationships, broken hearted-ness, and even death that people decide to learn who they are as individuals." That is their why.

When a person finally reaches the point where they cannot dodge the truth about themselves anymore, the weight of their experiences begins reshaping their identity. Sometimes it happens slowly, over months or years. Other times it feels like everything collapses in a single moment. But regardless of the pace, the breaking always produces a revealing. What they were hiding surfaces. What they avoided becomes undeniable. And what they thought made them strong is exposed as fragile. God often allows these moments because the version of themselves they were holding onto was never the one He intended for them to become.

When the truth finally comes to the surface, a person is faced with a decision they can no longer outrun. Truth demands a response. Some people try to gather the pieces of their old identity and rebuild what God is trying to tear down. Others try to outrun the discomfort by distracting themselves with busyness, relationships, achievements, or anything that makes them feel in control again. But the ones who grow are the ones who allow the truth to sit with them long enough to reshape them. They let God speak into the emptiness instead of trying to fill it themselves. They stop defending who they were and begin listening for who they are becoming. This is where transformation truly begins, not just in the breaking but in the surrender that follows it.

Now, to be fair, it is possible that the change in the old friend did not come about through negative experiences, but those people are rare. Everyone has negative experiences. Odds are, there were things that happened where they came to the realization of God and their need of Him. Recognizing that you need God, when you do not have Him is the greatest negative thing anyone can experience. Even Jesus lamented, "My God, My God, why have You forsaken me?" (Matthew 27:46, Mark 15:34) when He experienced separation from God whilst covered in our sin.

That moment of discovery, when you realize your strength is not enough and your strategies cannot hold you together, is often the doorway God uses to draw you back to Himself. You come to the end of your own ability, not because God abandoned you, but because He allowed your self-made foundations to collapse. It is in that collapse that clarity forms. You finally see where you are, who you have become, and how deeply you need the One who never changes. Pain turns into a teacher, and the lesson is simple. You were never meant to live without God in the first place.

When relationships are not solidly grounded in an altruistic love, a godly love, people will eventually find themselves in a pit of loneliness and/or despair. This is normal because love only comes from God. God is love (1 John 4:8).

It is normal simply because it is common to experience the consequences of our choices, not because it is right. But just because it is common, that does not mean it is the way it must be. When people get to a place of loneliness or despair, those dark places that damaging relationships lead us, they begin to put up all sorts of barriers that keep people as far away as possible from their hearts. There is a risk and reward on the table when it comes to getting close to someone or allowing someone to get close to you.

Those barriers may feel like safety, but they quietly change how a person navigates the world. Isolation becomes a reflex. Independence becomes armor. Even kindness feels risky because it asks for openness. Over time, a person stops noticing the difference between protecting their heart and imprisoning it. The defenses that once seemed wise start working against them, shutting out not only harmful people but healthy ones as well. This is why many never experience the fullness of love God offers; the walls built to survive heartbreak end up muting the very healing God is trying to bring. Until those walls are acknowledged for what they are, they will keep shaping a person's life without their permission.

It is in these moments that a person begins learning how to live defensively rather than relationally. The heart becomes something to manage instead of something to offer, something to guard at all costs instead of something to share under God's covering. People start developing survival behaviors that feel protective but end up becoming prisons. Silence becomes safer than honesty. Isolation becomes easier than vulnerability. Even joy begins to feel dangerous because joy requires openness, and openness feels like a threat.

What most don't realize is that the walls they build to keep pain out also prevent healing from getting in. You can't selectively block emotions. The same barriers that keep heartbreak away also keep comfort away. The same defenses that stop betrayal also stop intimacy. The same distance that protects your heart from people also distances your heart from God. That is why so many people who believe in God still struggle to trust Him; they have never learned how to let anyone close without fear.

This is why spiritual growth often feels uncomfortable at first. God does not violate your boundaries, but He does press gently against the walls you've constructed, not to expose you but to free you. He understands why your defenses exist. He saw the betrayal. He saw the abandonment. He saw the moment your trust collapsed. But He also knows that you cannot experience the fullness of His love while living behind the barricades built by past pain.

Love must be allowed in before it can flow out. Healing must be received before identity can be restored. God draws near, not to take something from you, but to return to you what the world has stolen. He approaches the heart not as a thief but as a surgeon, not to break in but to repair. And in that repair, intimacy with Him becomes possible again — an intimacy that becomes the foundation for every other relationship you have.

When someone owns a building and they have something that they cherish what you find is that they purchase an alarm. Thieves plot, plan, and pursue ways to infiltrate every lock and security check that has been set up. They work to disable every laser and bypass every guard just to reach the valuables. The most precious thing you own is at risk to theft for the purposes of misuse toward someone else's benefit.

Due to this possibility, losing the thing you value most, then, becomes the thing that causes you to center your actions and everyday lifestyle around protecting it. I believe that this is how we treat God when it comes to letting Him have our hearts. He should be the thing we hold most valuable and do all we can to protect our relationship with Him by keeping, and turning, far away from sin. Instead, we treat God as if he is the thief attempting to steal from us.

This misunderstanding shifts the entire relationship a person has with God. Instead of approaching Him with trust, they approach Him with suspicion. Instead of receiving His guidance, they brace themselves for loss. They try to manage God the same way they manage people who have hurt them, expecting Him to demand more than He gives. But God is not trying to take anything that leads to life. He is trying to free a person from what keeps them bound. Until the heart sees God as the giver instead of the taker, it will keep resisting the very presence that was meant to heal it.

Because of the damage that has been done to you in relationships you build all sorts of walls and shields around your heart to protect it. No one is going to reach it once you bury the vault that houses it. And then you treat God as if He is some criminal trying to infiltrate every lock you have set up. As if He's going to disable every laser and bypass every metaphorical guard you have constructed to keep Him from the thing you value most, your heart. Yet, your heart is not the thing God wants to take at all. While you try to save your heart from heartache, pain, and despair, God desires to give you a clean heart (Psalm 51:10). A new heart. His own.

Shift Your Focus

In Psalm 51:3-4 David writes to God, "For I know my transgressions, and my sin is always before me. Against You, You only, have I sinned and done what is evil in Your sight; so, You are right in Your verdict and justified when You judge." He later goes on to ask God to create in him a clean heart, to renew a steadfast spirit, for God to not turn away from him, and grant him a willing spirit for sustainment (v10-12). This is the key for us today!

David did not choose to dwell on and live in his despair. He chose to admit his failures and shift his focus from his sin to the character and power of the Father. He did not act as if he did not sin by hiding it; He laid his shortcomings at the throne of the Father as bare as Adam was when God made him. Then, he refocused his view on the capability and character of God.

God wants to clean your heart! God wants to leave your sin nailed to the altar of Calvary's cross! God wants you to receive more of Him, for only He is clean. You receive His cleanliness, His Spirit, as He cleans you up. This ensures that the shame, failure, and pain that comes from your sin does not overtake you and create barriers between you and God, as it did with God and Adam. You cannot live in despair and worship God at the same time!

David continues this sentiment throughout the entirety of Psalm 107. It starts off with, "Give thanks to the Lord, for He is good; His love endures forever" (v1). He immediately dials in on the goodness of God. David then gives instructions to those that have been redeemed to tell their stories. Throughout the entire Psalm, David explains short stories of the redeemed, how they were steeped in sin and darkness. In their darkness God, like a loving Father, gave a dwelling place (v7), brought them out and broke away their chains (v14), delivered them from their destructions, (v20), and guides them to their desired haven (v30). Each time, David lets us know what the appropriate response is, to God's loving intrusion.

Four times, David writes, "Oh that men would give thanks to the Lord for His goodness. And for His wonderful works to the children of men!" (v8, 15, 21, 31). Then, he rejoices from verse 32 all the way to 42 about the character of and power of God! Again, you cannot live in despair and worship God at the same time! Clean water can come out of a dirty faucet. Just because your outside may look like what you have been through does not mean that the cleansing power of God has not taken place on the inside of you!

Like David, you can shift your focus from what You are experiencing, or have experienced, and all the negative aspects of it. Understand that God is in control and living in His presence is more about you needing Him than Him needing you. He desires you, a personal and deep relationship with you. So do not dwell on your shortcomings. Be honest to your Father, God, and lay your sins at His feet. He already knows, so do not try to hide it. Then, worship Him pure and clean as He continues to work in and through you. Despite your circumstances, He is good. Oh, that [you] would give thanks to the Lord for His goodness. And for His wonderful works to work in [you]. "Whoever is wise will observe these things. And they will understand the lovingkindness of the Lord" (v43).

Now, What?

We've already discussed that in order to hear from God you must first have His Spirit. You must accept Jesus' salvation. God has no reason to communicate anything extra about your life or His plans if you have not received the Holy Spirit because the Holy Spirit is God's messenger. Let's take it a step further.

In order to actively live out a life of love, after receiving salvation, you must learn what God has to say in His Word about how to handle situations and circumstances when they arrive in your life. God certainly has a lot to say, specifically, about subjects in reference to how He feels about things that occur. Additionally, principally, God has a lot to say about how to handle things in your everyday life.

Through time with God, personal study, and your spiritual community the Father reveals His mind and thoughts to you. That's the easy part. The hard part is subjecting your own thoughts to compare them with His and following Jesus' footsteps when He said, "Father if it be Your will take this cup from Me. But not my will, Your will be done" (Luke 22:42).

It means taking your will, your thoughts, your desires, comparing them to God's and making the decision to choose His will, His thoughts, and His desires for yourself. You read and study the Bible to store God's word in your mind and heart. Then, it is through the Holy Spirit that God communicates Himself. We know this to be true because His Word tells us, "But when He, the Spirit of truth, comes, He will guide you into all the truth. He will not speak on His own; He will speak only what He hears, and He will tell you what is yet to come" (John 16:13). Thus, the only question which remains is, "What will you choose to do because of it?"

"It means taking your will, your thoughts, your desires, comparing them to God's and making the decision to choose His will, His thoughts, and His desires for yourself."

Chapter 4
The Greatest Love

Jesus prayed, "Father, I want those you have given Me to be with Me where I am, and to see My glory, the glory You have given Me because You loved Me before the creation of the world" (John 17:24). This is my personal prayer for you, for anyone you know, and everyone in existence. The reality of it all is that not everyone will recognize God's grace and accept His offer of salvation. The beautiful thing is, it is still offered to everyone and can be accepted at any time.

What if I told you that death does not really exist? You would probably say that I was crazy. But I assure you that death certainly does not exist. I mean, you cannot use negative indicators to describe something that does exists. But when you describe "death", you are really describing what is not there… life. Let me explain.

There are literally no visible signs of death. When someone "dies", there are simply no signs of life. Contrarily, there are visible signs of life. How does this relate to Christianity?

Well, I am glad you asked.

One thing many people do not fully understand is that everyone will spend eternity somewhere. The autonomy to live somewhere hot or not is totally up to each person. That being said, the real meaning of death and life needs to be hashed out.

When God told Adam not to eat from the tree of the knowledge of good and evil He added, "for when you eat from it you will certainly die" (Genesis 2:17). Satan confused Eve by twisting God's words stating, "You won't certainly die" (Genesis 3:4). Eve ate from the tree, shared with Adam and the rest is history. Neither Eve nor Adam died, literally.

Instead, they both lived long lives and raised a family. The only thing that changed when the two sinned was that they were separated from God. Most Christians would say, "They became spiritually dead" but what does that really mean? Let us fast forward a bit and then come back to Genesis.

Death And Life

Describe the word "death". While we are at it, why don't we list some of the more common descriptions:

- Someone is not breathing

- Someone is not moving

- Someone is not making sounds

Death is a word used to describe the absence of life. You cannot describe death because there are no visible signs of death. When someone is dead, there are simply no signs of life. Hold on to this thought.

In John 10, Jesus is explaining His immense love. He speaks, "I came that [everyone] may have life, and have it to the full (v10). Jesus would not offer something that the recipient already has, so why would He offer "...life and have it to the full", unless they did not have it? The word "and" is a conjunction denoting two separate thoughts together. Therefore, having life and [having life] to the full are two separate things. Yet, you cannot have life to the full without first having life. This is evidenced in Paul's writings in Ephesians 2 when he pens:

"But God, who is rich in mercy, because of His great love with which He loved us, even when we were dead in trespasses, made us alive together with Christ (by grace you have been saved), and raised us up together, and made us sit together in the heavenly places in Christ Jesus..." (Ephesians 2:4-6)

Jesus states, "I am the way, the truth, and the life. No one comes to the Father except through Me" (John 14:6). Now, we have just discussed how death is a word used to describe the absence of life. In comparison, Jesus Christ describes Himself as "Life". Therefore, it can be adequately stated that death really is a word used to describe the absence of Christ.

Considering that, when God told Adam he would certainly die if he ate from the tree of the knowledge of good and evil what He really meant was, "Adam, if you sin you will be separated from Me. You will... die. You will not have... life." In laymens terms, God was saying, "You will lose your connection to Me."

The point of it all is this: You do not deserve God's love. None of us do. There is nothing any of us could do to deserve it. There is nothing we could do to be worthy of His love or to earn or keep it. Nevertheless, He gives us His love. He gave us His Son, and He offers us salvation despite us not deserving it, despite us not being able to earn it, and despite us not being worthy of it. Though God knows of our sins and transgressions, His loves is such that He treats us as if His love is ignorant of our sins and transgressions. That is the heart of the Gospel. That is the entire message!

He loves you enough to give you His perfection in exchange for your imperfections, in exchange for every sin past, present, and future, in exchange for every lie you have ever told, in exchange for everything you have ever stole, in exchange for every wrongdoing you have committed, and in exchange for every malicious thought. God loves you enough to give you Himself, His Son, and His Spirit!

Ignorant love is something that He gives us but we struggle to give to others. By getting to know God personally and allowing ourselves to become more like Him we put ourselves in position to be better capable of giving God's ignorant love to others and better able to love others despite the things they have done. If everyone did that, how much more rewarding would relationships be? But the truth of us as humans is that not everyone will.

It starts with you, individually, and spreads through your interactions with others as you become more intentional to look at people with the compassion and joy that is Jesus Christ. I will leave you with this... This is not something you have to do but if you never begin, how many fewer people in the world will see the light, and love, of Jesus Christ?

P.I.G.E.E.

Father, God, You are magnificent in all of Your ways. In Your magnificence, You took off the glory of Jesus Christ and clothed Him in flesh. Thank You! I pray that everyone reading this book recognizes the weight You carried, acknowledges Your sacrifices, and receives Your grace and salvation. May they endure a relationship that is PROGRESSIVE, infinitely moving forward toward Christ's likeness. May they be INTENIONAL, making personal effort to grow and develop into His likeness through study and relationship with You. May they be GOAL-ORIENTED, keeping their eyes on You, Your kingdom, and Your will being done in their lives. May their learning and growth in their relationship with You produce EXPERIENCES where they see, hear, and follow You with deep clarity and focus. Lastly, may they freely and boldly EXPRESS those experiences to others as they go and make disciples, teaching all that You have commanded, as if they are ignorant of anyone's sins. By the power of Your Son Jesus, I humbly ask and pray these things. Hallelujah. Amen.

"Though God knows of our sins and transgressions, His love is such that He treats us as if His love is ignorant of our sins and transgressions. That is the heart of the Gospel. That is the entire message."

"Love... ignorantly."

- Randy L. Reynolds

With Gratitude,

Thank you for allowing me to share this message of God's intentional, ignorant love with you. I pray it has challenged, encouraged, and awakened something new within your spirit.

This is only the beginning. In The Difference Maker, we'll dive deeper into practically understanding and experiencing relationship with God.

Until then, stay faithful, stay intentional, and love… ignorantly.

— Randy L. Reynolds

www.ingramcontent.com/pod-product-compliance
Lightning Source LLC
Chambersburg PA
CBHW051737040426
42447CB00008B/1186